For the great students of St. Mary's, who introduced me to the word 'sarsaparilla'.

Alan St. Jean

© Text copyright 2020 Alan St. Jean.
© Illustrations copyright 2020 Alan St. Jean.
All rights reserved. First Edition.
Published by Oren Village, LLC, Sunbury, Ohio.
For information or permission to reproduce, please contact
alanstjean@gmail.com or write to Alan St. Jean, PO Box 900, Sunbury, Ohio 43074.
Text set in Anime Ace 2.0.
Cover design by Lilla Hangay. Illustrations were digitally rendered.

Names:
St. Jean, Alan, author.
Title:
Little Billy / by Alan St. Jean.
Description:
First edition. | Sunbury, Ohio : Oren Village, LLC, [2020] | Series: The young authors collection ; v. 2. | Audience: children. | Summary: A young cowboy walks into a saloon in Tumbleweed to order a sarsaparilla (which is root beer for those, like the author, who might be wondering). He is confronted by the biggest, smelliest, ugliest cowboy to ever roam the old west when the giant man refers to him as 'little'. Insecurities turn into laughter capped with a surprising ending in this...yes...it's a western.--Publisher.
Identifiers:
ISBN: 978-1-7333020-1-2
Subjects:
LCSH: Cowboys--Juvenile fiction. | Body size--Juvenile fiction. | Physical-appearance-based bias--Juvenile fiction. | Self-perception--Juvenile fiction. | Western stories. | Children's stories. | CYAC: Cowboys--Fiction. | Body size--Fiction. | Self-perception--Fiction. | West (U.S.)--Fiction. | LCGFT: Western fiction. | Picture books.
Classification:
LCC: PZ7.S14245 L58 2020 | DDC: [Fic]--dc23

# Little Billy

by Alan St. Jean

The Young Authors Collection • Volume 2

HORSE -N- WAGON...CHAINS A DRAGGIN'...

SPURS ARE CHANGIN'...LITTLE BILLY'S COME TO TOWN.
Salloon
Jeb's
Hank

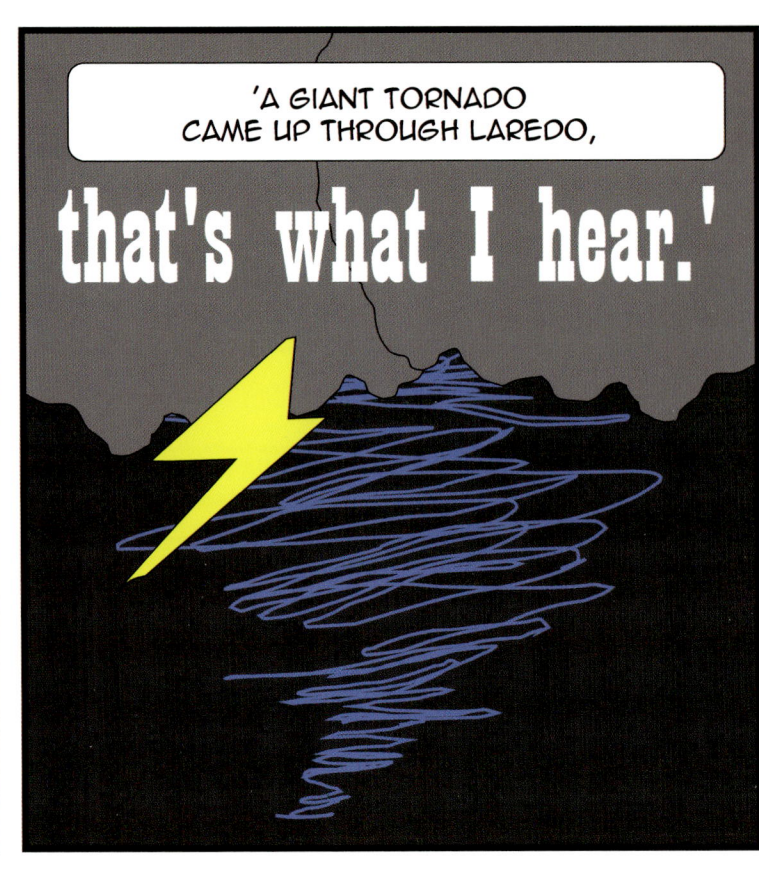

THE THREE BOYS OF A FEATHER CELEBRATED TOGETHER WITH A a great big hug!

LITTLE BILLY GAVE A SHOUT AS HIS EYES POPPED OUT, like a bug!

THERE, THEY DECIDED TO NEVER BE DIVIDED. THEY HAD TO FIND the mama.

# HELPFUL HINTS
(DON'T WORRY, LITTLE BILLY AND HIS FRIENDS WILL HELP AS YOU GO.)

## WHEN YOU WRITE:
ADD DETAILS, LIKE:
- *WHAT IS YOUR CHARACTER DOING?
- *WHY ARE THEY DOING IT?
- *HOW ARE THEY FEELING?

## WHEN YOU DRAW:
*DRAW YOUR PICTURE WITH A PENCIL FIRST SO YOU CAN MAKE CHANGES EASILY.
*THEN, COLOR IT!
(THAT'S HOW ILLUSTRATORS DO IT)
*ALSO, ADD DETAILS! SHOW THE SURROUNDINGS. BE CREATIVE!

## ARE YOU READY TO START??

# LET'S MEET YOUR CHARACTER

IN THIS SCENE, DRAW A NICE, BIG PICTURE OF YOUR CHARACTER. BE SURE TO USE A LOT OF DETAIL BECAUSE WE'RE INTRODUCING THEM TO THE READER. THIS IS THEIR PHYSICAL APPEARANCE.

IN THE BUBBLE BOX, TELL US TWO THINGS ABOUT YOUR CHARACTER. ARE THEY GOOD, OR BAD? ARE THEY HAPPY, OR SAD? ARE THEY SILLY, OR ARE THEY SNEAKY? THINGS LIKE THAT. THIS HELPS US INDERSTAND YOUR CHARACTER'S PERSONALITY.

**Thing one:**

**Thing two:**

# LET'S START THE STORY: BEGINNING

USE THE BUBBLE BOX TO WRITE THE BEGINNING OF YOUR STORY, THEN DRAW A PICTURE TO BRING YOUR WORDS TO LIFE. MAKE SURE YOU DRAW THEIR SURROUNDINGS, TOO. FOR EXAMPLE, IF THEY'RE IN A JUNGLE, DRAW TREES AND JUNGLE STUFF. IT'S CALLED THE SETTING. DETAILS ARE WHAT MAKE PICTURES AWESOME! DON'T TRY TO DRAW LIKE ANYONE ELSE, JUST DRAW THE WAY YOU DRAW, IT'S YOUR STYLE AND IT IS GOOD ENOUGH! YOU'RE AN ILLUSTRATOR!

One day,

# PLOT: THE BIG 'WHY'

WHAT HAPPENS NEXT IN YOUR STORY? DRAW THE SCENE HERE. IN THE BUBBLE BOX, EXPLAIN WHAT IS HAPPENING AND TELL US WHY THE CHARACTER IS DOING WHAT THEY ARE DOING.

Then,

# CONFLICT: SOMETHING GOES WRONG

THINGS ARE ABOUT TO GET BAD. CONFLICT HELPS MAKE A STORY MORE INTERESTING. BASED ON WHAT'S HAPPENING IN THE STORY, TELL US WITH A PICTURE AND WITH YOUR WORDS WHAT HAS GONE WRONG FOR YOUR CHARACTER. ALSO, TELL US HOW THE CHARACTER FEELS ABOUT THE CONFLICT.

Suddenly,

# MORE CONFLICT!

OH, NO! AS IF THINGS WEREN'T BAD ENOUGH, SOMETHING ELSE WENT WRONG! THIS IS AWFUL! WAIT A MINUTE. HMMM. NO, THIS IS FUN!

Things got worse because

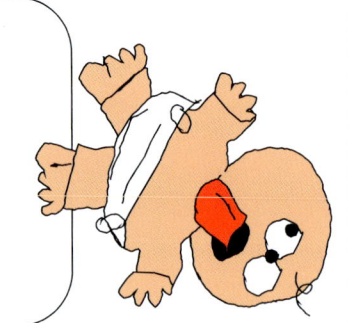

# RESOLUTION

CONFLICT IS FUN IN A STORY, BUT WE NEED TO FIX THE PROBLEM SO THAT THE READER FEELS SATISFIED AT THE END. IF WE DON'T FIX THE PROBLEM, THE STORY IS NO FUN TO READ.
DRAW A PICTURE AND USE YOUR WORDS TO TELL US WHAT HAPPENS NEXT THAT CAN FIX THE PROBLEMS FOR YOUR CHARACTER. DO THEY FIGURE OUT A WAY TO FIX THEIR OWN PROBLEM?
OR, DID SOMEONE ELSE SAVE THEM?

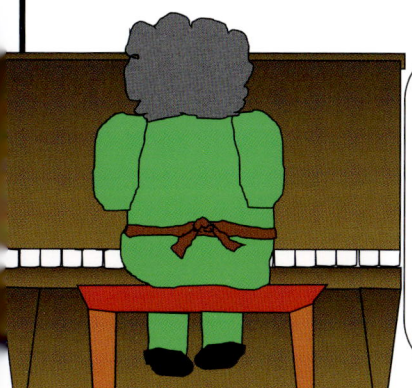

The day was saved when

# ENDING

WE'RE NOT SIMPLY GOING TO SAY 'THE END' HERE...THAT'S SILLY AND MAKES THE STORY WAY TOO SHORT. LET'S HAVE FUN WITH THIS. IN THE BUBBLE BOX, TELL US WHAT YOUR CHARACTER LEARNED FROM THEIR EXPERIENCE. THEN, DRAW A PICTURE THAT SHOWS WHAT BECAME OF THEM IN THE FUTURE! DID THEY BECOME FAMOUS? DID THEY GET MARRIED? I KNOW...EWWW!

Our character learned